DELANEY
STREET
PRESS

Women Say the
Wisest Things

Women Say the Wisest Things

A Concise Treasury of Women's Wisdom

by Mary Carlisle Beasley

DELANEY STREET PRESS
Nashville, TN: (800) 256-8584

ISBN 1-58334-076-9

The ideas expressed in this book are not, in all cases, exact quotations, as some have been edited for clarity and brevity. In all cases, the author has attempted to maintain the speaker's original intent. In some cases, material for this book was obtained from secondary sources, primarily print media. While every effort was made to ensure the accuracy of these sources, the accuracy cannot be guaranteed. For additions, deletions, corrections or clarifications in future editions of this text, please write DELANEY STREET PRESS.

Printed in the United States of America
Cover Design by Bart Dawson
Typesetting & Page Layout by Criswell Freeman

1 2 3 4 5 6 7 8 9 10 • 00 01 02 03 04 05 06

ACKNOWLEDGMENTS

The author gratefully acknowledges the helpful support of Angela Beasley Freeman, Dick and Mary Freeman, Mary Susan Freeman, Jim Gallery, and the entire team of professionals at DELANEY STREET PRESS and WALNUT GROVE PRESS.

For Helen Williams,
a shining example of wisdom,
generosity, happiness,
and love

Table of Contents

A woman is like
a tea bag. You never
know how strong she
is until she gets
into hot water.

Eleanor Roosevelt

1

Courage

Life has a way of testing all of us. Just when we think we have things all figured out, another question presents itself. The quotations in this book can help provide answers to those questions.

Using the words of some of history's wisest women, these pages are intended to encourage the reader with concise but power-packed gems of womanly wisdom.

If you're facing a bump in the road, or if you know someone who is, consider sage advice that follows. In this chapter, courageous women remind us that determination serves us well in good times and bad.

Courage is the price
that life exacts for
granting peace. The
soul that knows it not
knows no release from
little things.

Amelia Earhart

Do not borrow trouble
by dreading tomorrow.
It is the dark menace
of the future that
makes cowards
of us all.

Dorothy Dix

Fear brings out the worst
in everybody.

Maya Angelou

Courage is fear that has said
its prayers.

Dorothy Bernard

Women must not accept; they must
challenge. They must not be awed
by that which has been built up around
them; they must have reverence for the
things inside themselves that struggle
for expression.

Margaret Sanger

Become so wrapped
up in something
that you forget
to be afraid.

Lady Bird Johnson

I've always grown from my challenges,
from the things that didn't work out.
That's when I've really learned.
Carol Burnett

It takes as much courage to have
tried and failed as it does to have
tried and succeeded.
Anne Morrow Lindbergh

Pain nourishes courage. You can't be
brave if you've only had wonderful
things happen to you.
Mary Tyler Moore

When you get into a really tight place and everything goes against you, till it seems as though you could not hang on a minute longer, never give up then; for that is just the place and time that the tide will turn.

Harriet Beecher Stowe

To get it right, be born with luck or else make it. Never give up. Get the knack of getting people to help you and also pitch in yourself.

Ruth Gordon

There is no chance, no destiny,
no fate, that can hinder or control
the firm resolve of a determined soul.
Ella Wheeler Wilcox

Challenges make you discover things
about yourself that you never really
knew. They're what make you stretch
and go beyond the norm.
Cicely Tyson

Luck? I don't know anything
about luck. I've never banked on it and
I'm afraid of people who do. Luck to me
is something else: Hard work — and
realizing what is opportunity
and what isn't.
Lucille Ball

The one predominant
duty is to find one's
work and do it.

Charlotte Perkins Gilman

With hard work, the
world is your oyster.
You can do anything
you want to do.
I learned that at
a young age.

Chris Evert Lloyd

One of the things I learned the hard way was that it doesn't pay to get discouraged. So always keep busy and make optimism a way of life.

Lucille Ball

I am not afraid
of storms for I am
learning how to
sail my ship.

Louisa May Alcott

2

Friends

The following quotations remind us that friends must be treasured and cultivated. In happy times, friends are one of life's great luxuries; in times of struggle, they are a necessity. On sunny days, friends share laughter and hope; on cloudy days, they share courage.

A single true friend can serve as protection against the storms of life. With two or three genuine friends, a woman can face almost anything.

Friendship with one-
self is all-important,
because without it,
one cannot be friends
with anyone else
in the world.

Eleanor Roosevelt

I can trust my friends.
They force me to
examine myself, and
they encourage
me to grow.

Cher

A friend is one who
   sees through you and still
      enjoys the view.
         Wilma Askinas

Happy is she to whom, in the
   maturer season of life, there remains
      one tried and constant friend.
         Anna Letitia Barbauld

The best time to make friends
   is before you need them.
         Ethel Barrymore

Best friend,
my wellspring in
the wilderness!

George Eliot

Trouble is a sieve
through which we
sift our acquaintances.
Those too big to
pass through are
our friends.

Arlene Francis

A friend can tell you things
you don't want to tell yourself.
Frances Ward Weller

Only friends will tell you the truths
you need to hear to make
your life bearable.
Francine Du Plessix Gray

Surely we ought to prize
those friends on whose principles
and opinions we may
constantly rely.
Hannah Farnham Lee

We have really no absent friends.
Elizabeth Bowen

The most beautiful discovery
true friends make is that they can
grow separately without growing apart.
Elizabeth Foley

She is a friend. She gathers the
pieces and gives them back to me
in all the right order.
Toni Morrison

It's the friends
that you can call
up at 4 a.m.
that matter.

Marlene Dietrich

Each friend represents
a world in us, a world
possibly not born until
they arrive, and it is
only by this meeting
that a new world
is born.

Anaïs Nin

My friends have made the story
of my life. In a thousand ways they
have turned my limitations into
beautiful privileges and enabled me
to walk serene and happy in the
shadow cast by my deprivation.
Helen Keller

The balm of life — a kind
and faithful friend.
Mercy Otis Warren

It is wise to pour the oil of refined
politeness on the mechanism
of friendship.
Colette

You can keep your friends
by not giving them away.
Mary Pettibone Poole

Friendship takes time.
Agnes Repplier

Silences make the real conversations
between friends.
Margaret Lee Runbeck

If you want to be listened to,
   you should put in time listening.
                              Marge Piercy

Acquaintances ask about our
   outward life; friends ask about
         our inner life.
                  Marie von Ebner-Eschenbach

Intimacies between women often
go backwards, beginning in revelations
      and ending in small talk.
                        Elizabeth Bowen

What I cannot love,
I overlook. That is
friendship.

Anaïs Nin

The person who
treasures friends
is solid gold.

Marjorie Holmes

There's no friend like someone
who has known you since you were five.
Anne Stevenson

True friends are the ones who
really know you but love you anyway.
Edna Buchanan

My true friends have always
given me that supreme proof of
devotion, a spontaneous aversion
to the man I love.
Colette

$\underline{3}$

Love

Love is the little four-letter word that changes everything. On the pages that follow, wise women share the kind of wisdom that comes straight from the heart.

Love yourself first and everything else falls into line. You really have to love yourself to get anything done in this world.

Lucille Ball

Love is a great beautifier.
Louisa May Alcott

Whoever loves true life,
will love true love.
Elizabeth Barrett Browning

Love involves a peculiar
unfathomable combination of
understanding and misunderstanding.
Diane Arbus

Nobody has ever measured,
   not even poets, how much
   the heart can hold.
                        Zelda Fitzgerald

Love is a game that two can play
   and both win.
                        Eva Gabor

Love is a
multiplication.

Marjory Stoneman Douglas

To love deeply in one direction
makes us more loving in all others.
Madame Swetchine

Love dies only when growth stops.
Pearl Buck

Accustom yourself continually to
make many acts of love, for they
enkindle and melt the soul.
St. Teresa of Avila

Love is not a state,
it is a direction.

Simone Weil

The story of love is not
important. What is
important is that one
is capable of love. It is
perhaps the only
glimpse we have
of eternity.

Helen Hayes

The strongest evidence of love
is sacrifice.

Carolyn Fry

Great loves too must be endured.

Coco Chanel

A woman who is loved
always has success.
Vicki Baum

A good marriage is like an
oriental rug, with all those
patterns in it.
Helen Fisher

Love doesn't just sit there,
like stone; it has to be made,
like bread, remade all the time,
made new.
Ursula K. Le Guin

Both of us are groping and
a little lost. But we are together.
Anne Morrow Lindbergh

All love that has not friendship
for its base is like a mansion
built upon the sand.
Ella Wheeler Wilcox

Ideally, couples need three lives:
one for him, one for her, and
one for them together.
Jacqueline Bisset

The best and most beautiful things
in the world cannot be seen or
even touched. They must be felt
with the heart.

Helen Keller

Him that I love, I wish to be
free — even from me.

Anne Morrow Lindbergh

Love will not always linger longest
with those who hold it in
too clenched a fist.

Alice Duer Miller

The best proof
of love is
trust.

Dr. Joyce Brothers

There is only one terminal dignity — love.

Helen Hayes

Until I truly loved,
I was alone.

Caroline Norton

The giving of love is
      an education in itself.
Eleanor Roosevelt

Love conquers all except
      poverty and toothaches.
Mae West

When you come right
down to it, the secret
of having it all
is loving it all.

Dr. Joyce Brothers

To love is to
receive a glimpse
of heaven.

Karen Sunde

4

Faith

When life becomes a struggle, wise women find comfort through faith. Faith is born in an optimistic spirit, nurtured in a wise heart, carefully cultivated each day, and then generously shared with others.

Faith is the foundation that cannot be shaken, the light that leads ever forward. It is the anchor that holds fast and protects us until the storm clouds have cleared.

Faith is a spiritual
spotlight that
illuminates
one's path.
Helen Keller

Faith is an activity. It is something that has to be applied.

Corrie ten Boom

Faith can put a candle in
      the darkest night.
Margaret Sanger

Seeds of faith are always within us;
sometimes it takes a crisis to nourish
   and encourage their growth.
Susan L. Taylor

Faith is what makes life bearable.
Madeleine L'Engle

To have courage
for whatever
comes in life —
everything lies
in that.

Saint Teresa of Avila

Faith sees the invisible,
 believes the unbelievable,
 and receives the impossible.
Corrie ten Boom

Faith wears everyday clothes
 and proves herself in life's
 ordinary circumstances.
Bertha Munro

Faith is like radar that sees
 through the fog — the reality
 of things at a distance that the
 human eye cannot see.
Corrie ten Boom

Faith is the
key that fits the
door of hope.

Elaine Emans

Faith is the only known
cure for fear.

Lena Sadler

Keep your face to the sunshine
and you cannot see the shadows.

Helen Keller

God's gifts put man's
best gifts to shame.

Elizabeth Barrett Browning

There are no hopeless situations; there are only people who have grown hopeless.

Clare Boothe Luce

My recipe for life is
   not being afraid of myself.
                              Eartha Kitt

Nothing in life is to be feared.
   It is only to be understood.
                              Marie Curie

Without faith,
nothing is possible.
With it, nothing
is impossible.

Mary McLeod Bethune

Sad soul, take comfort
nor forget, the sunrise
never failed us yet.

Celia Thaxter

5

Happiness

Wise women understand that life is far too short to remain unhappy for long. Certainly, periods of sadness must be endured from time to time: This is the price we all must pay for living and loving. But periods of sadness should be nothing more than brief intermissions in the otherwise happy stories of our lives.

Ultimately, the great secret of life is to treasure it while it lasts. The following quotations tell how.

Cheerfulness, it would
appear, is a matter
which depends fully
as much on the state
of things within us
as on the state of
things without.

Charlotte Brontë

Happiness is a matter of one's
  most ordinary everyday mode of
consciousness: being busy, and lively,
  and unconcerned with self.
  Iris Murdoch

If only we'd stop trying to be happy,
  we could have a pretty good time.
  Edith Wharton

One must never look for happiness:
  one meets it by the way....
  Isabelle Eberhardt

Joy is what happens
to us when we allow
ourselves to recognize
how good things
really are.

Marianne Williamson

Happiness is good health
and a bad memory.
Ingrid Bergman

The greater part of happiness depends
on our dispositions and not
our circumstances.
Martha Washington

Happiness to me is enjoying
my friends and family.
Reba McEntire

There is only one happiness in life:
to love and be loved.
George Sand

This is happiness:
to be dissolved into
something complete
and great.

Willa Cather

Too many wish
to be happy before
becoming wise.

Suzanne Curchod Necker

Earth's crammed
with heaven.

Elizabeth Barrett Browning

Be happy.
It's one way of
being wise.

Colette

6

Attitude

Savvy women of all ages understand that despair is a poor counselor indeed. It has been correctly observed that attitude determines altitude: The better we think, the higher we fly. The words that follow can provide the kind of attitude adjustment that makes for a beautiful, safe, enjoyable flight.

Optimism is that
faith that leads
to achievement.
Nothing can be
done without hope
and confidence.

Helen Keller

If you think you can, you can.
And if you think you can't,
you're right.
Mary Kay Ash

No pessimist ever discovered the
secrets of the stars, or sailed to
an uncharted land, or opened a
new heaven to the human spirit.
Helen Keller

It is best to act with confidence,
no matter how little right
you have to it.
Lillian Hellman

There is nothing from the outside that can defeat any of us.

Margaret Mitchell

In the long run, we shape our lives
and we shape ourselves. The process
never ends until we die.
Eleanor Roosevelt

All times are beautiful for those
who maintain joy within them;
but there are no happy times for those
with disconsolate souls.
Rosalia Castro

The way in which we think of ourselves
has everything to do with how
our world sees us.

Arlene Raven

Happiness is not a matter of events;
it depends on the tides of the mind.

Alice Meynell

Reach high, for stars
lie hidden in your soul.
Dream deep, for every
dream precedes
the goal.

Pamela Vaull Starr

How very little can
be done under the
atmosphere
of fear.

Florence Nightingale

Act as if
it were impossible
to fail.

Dorthea Brande

Live as if you like
yourself, and it
may happen.

Marge Piercy

Everything is in the mind.
　　Knowing what you want is
　　the first step in getting it.
Mae West

You must do the thing
　　you think you cannot do.
Eleanor Roosevelt

A fool without fear is sometimes
　　wiser than an angel with fear.
Nancy Astor

It only seems as if
you are doing
something when
you're worrying.

Lucy Maud Montgomery

7

Life

Life is the work of art that each woman must fashion in her own way and with her own hands. As her life's work takes shape, each woman leaves her mark according to the way she lives. On the following pages, wise women reveal their secrets for creating a masterpiece.

Live with no time out.

Simone de Beauvoir

Nothing is so often irretrievably
missed as a daily opportunity.
Marie von Ebner-Eschenbach

Life hurries past, too strong to stop,
too sweet to loose.
Willa Cather

Nobody's gonna' live for you.
Dolly Parton

Life is what we make it. Always has been. Always will be.

Grandma Moses

Life is my college. May I graduate
well, and earn some honors!
Louisa May Alcott

See into life — don't just look at it.
Anne Baxter

As long as one keeps searching,
the answers will come.
Joan Baez

It is not enough to reach for
the brass ring. You must also enjoy
the merry-go-round.
Julie Andrews

Life never becomes a habit to me.
It's always a marvel.
Katherine Mansfield

What we are is God's gift to us.
What we become is our gift to God.
Eleanor Powell

Life is the raw material. We are the artisans.

Cathy Better

Life is either
a daring adventure
or nothing.
Helen Keller

8

All-purpose Advice

Margot Bennett writes, "As time passes, we all get better at blazing a trail through the thicket of advice." In this concluding chapter, we consider a thicket-full of savvy sayings from a collection of wise women. Enjoy!

It is never too late to
be what you might
have been.

George Eliot

Action is the antidote to despair.
Joan Baez

A good goal is like a strenuous
exercise – it makes you stretch.
Mary Kay Ash

If you want to accomplish the goals
of your life, you have to begin
with the Spirit.
Oprah Winfrey

Only I can change my life. No one can do it for me.

Carol Burnett

We can do no great things;
only small things with great love.

Mother Teresa

It is up to each of us to contribute
something to this sad and
wonderful world.

Eve Arden

We are all cremated equal.

Jane Ace

Give the world
the best you have, and
the best will come
back to you.

Madeline Bridges

Every woman is free to rise as far as she's able or willing, but the degree to which she thinks determines the degree to which she'll rise.

Ayn Rand

Life is about having to change and making the best of it, without knowing what's going to happen next.

Gilda Radner

Trouble is the common denominator of living, and it can be a blessing. Problems act like grindstones to smooth and polish us.

Ann Landers

It's nice to be successful,
   but nice isn't the essence of living.
         Struggle is.
                        Mary Tyler Moore

It's not the load that breaks you down;
   it's the way you carry it.
                        Lena Horne

Surely the consolation prize of old age is finding out how few things are worth worrying over.

Dorothy Dix

Each day, look for a
	kernel of excitement.
		Barbara Johnson

Talk happiness. The world is
	sad enough without your woes.
		Ella Wheeler Wilcox

Anger makes us all stupid.
		Johanna Spyri

An optimistic mind
is a healthy mind.

Loretta Young

Life does not have
to be perfect
to be wonderful.

Annette Funicello

The hardest thing you will ever do
is trust yourself.
Barbara Walters

It was my mother's belief — and
mine — to resist any
negative thinking.
Audrey Meadows

Misery is a communicable disease.
Martha Graham

All our lives,
we are preparing to be
something or somebody,
even if we don't
know it.

Katherine Anne Porter

Everybody must learn
this lesson somewhere:
It costs something to be
what you are.

Shirley Abbott

When I stand before God at the end of my life, I would hope that I would not have a single bit of talent left and could say, "I used everything you gave me."

Erma Bombeck

Sources

Sources

About the Author

Mary Carlisle Beasley is a writer who lives and works in Nashville, Tennessee and is the author of numerous books including several published by DELANEY STREET PRESS.

About
DELANEY STREET PRESS

DELANEY STREET PRESS publishes a series of books designed to inspire and entertain readers of all ages. DELANEY STREET books are distributed by Walnut Grove Press. For more information, please call 1-800-256-8584.